BIG MACHINES FOR BIG JOBS

BULLDOZERS ON THE JOB

NORWOOD HOUSE PRESS

RYAN JAMES

Cataloging-in-Publication Data

Names: James, Ryan.
Title: Bulldozers on the job / Ryan James.
Description: Buffalo, NY : Norwood House Press, 2026. | Series: Big machines for big jobs | Includes glossary and index.
Identifiers: ISBN 9781978573789 (pbk.) | ISBN 9781978573796 (library bound) | ISBN 9781978573802 (ebook)
Subjects: LCSH: Bulldozers--Juvenile literature.
Classification: LCC TA725.J359 2026 | DDC 629.225--dc23

Published in 2026 by
Norwood House Press
2544 Clinton Street
Buffalo, NY 14224

Designer: Rhea Magaro
Editor: Kim Thompson

Photo credits: Cover, p. 1 Stock Holm/Shutterstock.com; p. 3 surawach5/Shutterstock.com; p. 5 Photos SS/Shutterstock.com; p. 6 AButyrin 22/Shutterstock.com; p. 7 Vladimir Konstantinov/Shutterstock.com; p. 9 RobSt/Shutterstock.com; p. 10 Roman023_photography/Shutterstock.com; p. 11 Alexey_Rezvykh/Shutterstock.com; p. 12, 13 PRILL/Shutterstock.com; p. 15 Comaniciu Dan/Shutterstock.com; p. 16 Uud. N. Hudana/Shutterstock.com; p. 18 WILLIAM LUQUE/Shutterstock.com; p. 19 M2020/Shutterstock.com; p. 21 Poppy Pix/Shutterstock.com;

Printed in the United States of America

CPSIA compliance information: Batch #CSNHP26: For further information contact Norwood House Press at 1-800-237-9932.

TABLE OF CONTENTS

PARTS OF A BULLDOZER

Bulldozers are big machines.

They move on two **tracks**.

The front of a bulldozer has a **blade**. The blade is attached to the push frame.

The back of a bulldozer has a ripper.

WHAT DOES A BULLDOZER DO?

Bulldozers work on **construction** sites. They break through hard **surfaces**. They move dirt and other **materials**.

The blade digs, lifts, and pushes.

A straight blade does all kinds of pushing.

A U-blade moves big loads.

An S-blade **shreds**.

The ripper is like a claw. It goes deep in the ground. It breaks up hard soil. Then, the blade moves the loose dirt away.

The **operator** sits in the cab. The operator **controls** the push frame. The push frame makes the blade lift. It makes the blade move forward and back.

D 65P
09

BULLDOZER SAFETY

Is a bulldozer near you? Listen to an adult. Stay safe so nobody gets hurt.

Do not go near a bulldozer without **permission**. Sharp, moving parts can hurt people.

The operator has an important job.

Do not bother them while they work.

BULLDOZERS IN ACTION

Bulldozers are **vehicles** on the job. They get work done on the construction site!

GLOSSARY

blade (blade): a flat, sharp-edged tool for cutting

construction (kuhn-STRUHK-shuhn): related to building houses, roads, and other structures

controls (kuhn-TROHLZ): makes a machine work by pushing buttons and moving levers and switches

materials (muh-TEER-ee-uhlz): things needed for a project, such as rocks, dirt, or bricks

operator (AH-puh-ray-tur): a person whose job is to work a machine

permission (pur-MISH-uhn): being told it is okay to do something

shreds (shredz): tears or breaks something into small pieces

surfaces (SUR-fuh-sis): the outside or top layers of something that you can see and touch

tracks (traks): looping belts that help a vehicle move over rough ground

vehicles (VEE-i-kuhlz): machines used to move people or things from one place to another

THINKING QUESTIONS

1. What is the job of a bulldozer?
2. Name three parts of a bulldozer.
3. How is each type of blade different from the others?
4. How can you stay safe around a bulldozer?
5. Why are bulldozers important?

INDEX

ABOUT THE AUTHOR

Ryan James lives in the mountains of North Carolina where he goes hiking with his dog Bailey. He loves fly fishing, visiting farms in the area, and picking fresh produce. He has always enjoyed writing and wrote his first book as a teenager.